Original title:
Life's Big Questions, Answered by Cake

Copyright © 2025 Creative Arts Management OÜ
All rights reserved.

Author: Lorenzo Barrett
ISBN HARDBACK: 978-1-80566-227-3
ISBN PAPERBACK: 978-1-80566-522-9

The Crust of Consciousness

What is the meaning, ask we all,
Is it in frosting, or in a bowl?
A cake so sweet, with layers deep,
Says ponder not, just take a leap!

Baking brings wisdom, it's no debate,
With batter and eggs, we contemplate.
Whisking our troubles, icing our fears,
Each bite unveils, laughter and tears.

A Slice of Speculation

What's over the rainbow, and why's it there?
   Is it a cake that we all can share?
With sprinkles of joy and a cherry on top,
   Let's speculate while we eat and swap!

Do dreams rise high like soufflés in the air?
   Or fall, like crumbs, without a care?
A fork in the road, let's dig right in,
   To find that wisdom lies within!

Happiness in a Hot Oven

Where does the joy of life reside?
In the warmth of the oven, let hope collide!
A cake full of laughter, a dash of cheer,
Baking up smiles, bringing friends near.

Is happiness found in frosting so sweet?
Or in gathering round, sharing a treat?
Whisking away doubts, let them dissolve,
In layers of joy, our hearts evolve.

The Slice of the Soul

What makes us whole, what seals the deal?
Is it a cake, or is it our zeal?
A slice of wonder, perhaps a crumb,
Life's tasty secrets, let's not be glum!

The cake of existence, each flavor unique,
With every bite, the questions we seek.
So slice it up, enjoy the feast,
In cake and laughter, we are released!

Piecing Together the Unknown

What is the secret to happiness found?
Is it in frosting, or pie crust profound?
A slice of chocolate could lead you to bliss,
With sprinkles on top, how could you resist?

Questions arise like layers of cake,
Is frosting a must or just a mistake?
If life is a feast, then I shall partake,
With each tasty bite, a new path I'll make.

The Flavor of Understanding

Beneath the icing, what truths lie in wait?
A hint of vanilla, a tantalizing fate.
Does passion reside in a buttery crumb?
With each bashful chew, answers start to come.

Carrot or chocolate, what's the best plan?
Is there meaning in ganache, or just in the pan?
With every good forkful, I ponder and chew,
Maybe the essence is simply to stew.

Morsels of Meaning

In the oven of life, what do we bake?
A pie full of dreams, or a roll full of flake?
Is joy a warm cookie fresh out of the tray?
Or maybe a muffin, brightening the day?

Questions are crumbs that we scatter with glee,
A dash of confusion, just sprinkle and see.
Every bite offers a riddle to crack,
With laughter and cake, there's no looking back.

Layered Disputes

Why do we argue, oh so sweet?
Is it the frosting, or is it the heat?
Layers of cake stack high on a plate,
Who knew dessert could seal our fate?

Chocolate or vanilla, a classic fight,
With sprinkles and toppings, oh what a sight!
Arguments crumble like old bread rolls,
But sugar brings joy to our hungry souls.

The Eloquent Pastry

Tarts speak softly, their crusts quite neat,
Whispering secrets with every sweet treat.
Eclairs tell tales of cream and of flair,
While cupcakes giggle, their frosting to share.

A pie slice debates just how to be served,
Each flaky layer has flavors preserved.
With each bite we ponder, we laugh and we cheer,
As pastries join in, making problems unclear.

Sweet Solutions

When problems arise, we simply bake,
For cookies provide a delicious escape.
Mix up some laughter, a dash of delight,
With every sweet treat, our spirits ignite.

Brownies unite, no quarrels in sight,
Together we share, our friendship takes flight.
In a world full of chaos, icing is key,
Who knew solving issues could taste this creamy?

Of Flour and Fortune

Flour flies high as dreams take their shape,
Baking our wishes, there's no need to escape.
Fortune favors those with a whisk in their hand,
Creating sweet moments, oh isn't it grand?

Mixing the batter, we chuckle and grin,
In this kitchen of life, where messes begin.
So grab your spatula, let joy be your guide,
For in every good cake, together we bide.

The Bake that Binds

In an oven of thoughts, I found a treat,
Sugar and spice make worries retreat.
Frosting on top, flavors collide,
Each slice, a lesson, can't be denied.

Whisked dreams bubble, rise in a bowl,
Mix in some laughter, that's the goal.
Layers of joy stacked high on a plate,
Bite into wisdom, don't hesitate.

Decadent Dilemmas

Should I have chocolate or go for the pie?
Each bite feels like asking 'oh why, oh why?'
Sprinkles of doubt in every decision,
I'll frolic in frosting, it's my new vision.

Cake is a puzzle, with slices to share,
Questions dissolve with a dollop of care.
In sticky situations, don't fret or quake,
Just laugh and enjoy another slice of cake.

Crumbs of Clarity

Crumbs on the table tell tales of old,
Every morsel a story waiting to unfold.
I ponder my fancies, with cream on my chin,
The deeper I think, the thicker the spin.

With every zucchini bread, life seems less grim,
Counting my blessings, don't let chances slim.
In frosting and fondant, the answers reside,
Take a bite of the cake, let curiosity glide.

The Recipe of Reflection

A pinch of this and a dash of that,
Stirring up thoughts while wearing a hat.
In the mixing bowl, perplexities swirl,
Add some vanilla, let sanity twirl.

Bake at a temperature, just right and grand,
Sift through your heart with a gentle hand.
For every layer, a choice must be made,
Slice through confusion, let pleasures cascade.

The Pastry Parade of Thoughts

In the kitchen of wishes, they bake and they fry,
Cakes of ambition with frosting to fly.
Whisking up dreams with a cherry on top,
Do we laugh at the frosting, or dive in and stop?

Rolling pins ponder, they spin and they twirl,
What is the meaning of life in a swirl?
Sugar sprinkles rain down, oh what a sight,
Ask the brownies, they're wise, and polite.

Cookies and Contemplation

In the oven of thoughts, cookies crunch and smile,
Each bite a question that lingers a while.
Chocolate chips whisper secrets of fate,
Can fortune dwell in a cookie on a plate?

Milk's a sidekick with questions galore,
Dunking the truth, then asking for more.
Do we crunch on the answers or savor the dough?
Life's just a treat, if you share it, you'll glow.

The Sweet Paradox

Frosting covers doubts in a whipped cream disguise,
How can confusion be sweet to our eyes?
Layered with humor, this cake speaks so true,
Do we eat the whole thing or just savor a few?

Sprinkles on top, will they answer our fate?
Each bite's a riddle, let's chew or debate.
Is a slice of joy worth a crumb of despair?
In the oven of thought, does it matter what's fair?

Pies of Perspective

A pie on the window sill watches the street,
Filled with questions and laughter, oh what a treat!
Does a slice hold knowledge, or just cinnamon dreams?
When life gets flaky, it's better than it seems!

Apple or cherry, what's the wise choice?
In crust we confide, we all have a voice.
The laughter of pastry, it echoes and calls,
With every sweet bite, we break down the walls.

Sweetening the Complexities

Why is the sky so blue, my friend?
A slice of cake might help us bend.
With frosting bright and sprinkles gay,
We'll ponder more, then munch away.

What's the point of all this stress?
A cupcake's charm can surely bless.
With chocolate goo and icing swirls,
Let's trade our woes for sweetened pearls.

Are we but crumbs in this great feast?
Maybe though, we're all released.
With every bite a tiny cheer,
The answers rise—so bring the beer!

Does time move fast or slow, I ask?
A cake expires, that's its task.
Let's savor each delicious slice,
And laugh about our cake advice!

The Cake Conclusives

When faced with choices, big or small,
Just grab a fork and have a ball.
For cakes can teach us what to do,
Just follow frosting, it's tried and true!

If life's a puzzle, what's the piece?
A layered cake, it brings us peace.
With every bite, we gain a thought,
More frosting dreams, our answers sought.

What's the secret to happiness?
A cake with layers, no less, no mess.
With every crumb, there's joy we find,
In whipped delight, we're intertwined.

What's the meaning of it all, dear friend?
Why not a cake with zest, to blend?
With laughter shared and crumbs to spare,
The truths come out while sweets we share.

Wisdom Whipped

When pondering life's ridiculous feats,
Let's whip some cream for our sweet retreats.
With butter and sugar, we'll mix and blend,
The wisest answers, a cake will send.

Is it true that happiness is fleeting?
Or is it more like endless eating?
With forks in hand and friends galore,
Let's whip up joy, who could want more?

What happens when the candles burn?
A cake says it's not our turn.
With every flame a wish we bake,
Embrace the melt, let's not forsake!

Can laughter really heal the soul?
Pour on the ganache, let's be whole.
For thoughts are better shared with cake,
So here's to smiles and pie to make.

Edible Epiphanies

In search of wisdom, we may roam,
But cake's the path that leads us home.
With icing bright and flavors bold,
We'll find our truths that sweetly unfold.

Why does the universe feel so vast?
A slice of cake brings us to the past.
With crumbs of history on our plate,
We'll laugh and ponder, isn't it great?

What of the trials that make us grow?
Let's bake a cake and let love flow.
With every slice a story shared,
True epiphanies, joys declared.

Are we just meant to dance through time?
With flour dust and icing rhyme.
So here's to questions, big and small,
With cake in hand, we'll conquer all!

The Meringue Manifesto

What is truth, a fluffy puff,
With cream and sugar, never tough.
Whip it high, let doubts dissolve,
In every bite, mysteries resolve.

Is love just a cake, rich and sweet?
Layered, frosted, a tasty treat.
With each slice, we find our way,
Meringue dreams brightening the day.

Questions Baked in Time

Do cookies hold the answers clear,
To ages past that we revere?
Baking soda, both fresh and wise,
Leavening thoughts like pies in the skies.

Why do we yearn for chocolate's kiss?
In drizzle and glaze, we find our bliss.
A crumbly edge, a fudgey core,
In each sample, we crave for more.

Sweet Soliloquies

What's the meaning of a pie?
Fruits in harmony, oh so spry.
Baked in harmony, crusted tight,
Each forkful brings new delight.

Is frosting the crown of our lore?
A swirl of joy, a sugary score.
Whip it good, let laughter rise,
In every bite, a sweet surprise.

Crystallized Curiosities

Are sprinkles the stars of our fate?
Colorful wonders placed on a plate.
With each crunch, we bask in glee,
The universe twinkling, can't you see?

Could cupcakes unlock ancient riddles?
Filled with cream, each thought nibbled.
In the frosting, truths start to gleam,
Life's puzzles solved in a sugary dream.

The Dilemma Dessert

When chocolate calls, do I resist?
A slice of vanilla, too good to miss.
Do calories count if you're happy?
The crunch of sprinkles feels quite snappy.

Frosting swirls, a sugary fight,
Is one more bite wrong or just right?
With layers stacked, my worries fade,
Maybe cake is the answer I've made.

A slice of pie, a cherry on top,
In this sweet world, I never want to stop.
What's better than cake when you're feeling blue?
Perhaps the sprinkles hold wisdom too.

So when doubts bubble, and life seems a mess,
Remember this truth, it's simple, I guess:
A party of flavors while munching away,
Is the answer we seek — let's celebrate!.

Pondering with Pastry

In a crusty shell, deep thoughts reside,
Whipped cream dreams are hard to hide.
Do cupcakes know what dreams might say?
Each bite a riddle, what a fun buffet!

Creamy layers, sweet as can be,
Do muffins hold secrets just like me?
With every crumb, a question flows,
What if frosting never froze?

Between the layers of pastry delights,
Lies wisdom wrapped in sugary bites.
Do cookies consent to our sweet desire?
With each one cracked, does joy transpire?

So nibble slow, and ponder well,
In every treat, a story to tell.
With cake in hand, we can embrace,
The quirkiness of truth in this frosty space.

Cupcake Conundrums

Frosted wonders, do I dare share?
Or hoard these treasures, keeping them rare?
With sprinkles bright and flavors galore,
Life's little mysteries, I won't ignore.

Do birthdays matter if the cake's a flop?
Or does each slice win, no chance to drop?
With every dozen, a question unfurls,
Can sweets solve the chaos of this world?

Do mini delights hold giant dreams true?
Or are they just snacks for a whimsical view?
The icing's thick, like thoughts that circle,
Each cupcake offers joy like a twinkle.

Let's slice through the doubts, enjoy the ride,
With cupcakes guiding, there's nothing to hide.
For in frosty swirls lies the key, I deem,
That every cupcake holds a sweet little dream.

Savory Snippets of Insight

With quiche in hand and a pie on the side,
Can savory treats ever take you for a ride?
Do tarts hold knowledge, are they wise?
Or is it just butter that opens our eyes?

Bite into layers, and ponder away,
What does the dough really want to say?
Each flaky crust, a story unfolds,
In each morsel, a mystery, bold.

And pastries whisper secrets profound,
While chocolate ganaches spin thoughts around.
When seeking answers, do cookies comply?
Or are they just brittle when we wonder why?

So let's indulge and toss worries aside,
Savor each bite, take a whimsical stride.
In the pastry laughter, we find our way,
As savory snippets brighten the day.

The Custard Conundrum

What gives joy, oh sweet delight?
A bowl of custard, creamy white.
With every spoonful, thoughts all fade,
Is happiness just dessert well-made?

In life's turmoil, we seek our slice,
A tart or pudding, oh, how nice!
Questions rise like bubbles afloat,
Still, custard's here, let's share the boat.

Is there truth in sugar's embrace?
Is frosting proof of love's warm grace?
As custard drips, we ponder why,
Layers of joy, like pie on high.

Layered Reflections in Chocolate

In layers dark, we dive so deep,
Where answers hide and secrets keep.
Chocolate's richness, oh so bold,
Unwrap a truth that can't be sold.

Each slice reveals a different hue,
A question bites, what's up with you?
Does frosting mask the gooey fears,
Or sweeten up our fleeting years?

With every layer, laughter grows,
The riddles swirl like cocoa flows.
In chocolate's charm, we find our way,
To savor life, come what may.

Chewy Queries

What's chewy, gooey, never bland?
Cookies asking for a hand.
Bite into puzzling, crispy fate,
Do we chew softly, or just wait?

In each delicious, crispy treat,
A question forms, can we compete?
With flavors mixing, doubts arise,
Is chewing through the truth the prize?

With every crunch, a giggle peeks,
In baked goods, wisdom speaks.
So pipe your frosting, hug it tight,
We bake our answers every night.

The Sifted Surprises

What lurks beneath the flour's dust?
Mysteries in every crust.
As we sift through, crumbs take flight,
What's hidden there? A bite of light?

In every sprinkle, questions bloom,
A cupcake's worth dispels the gloom.
With sprinkles bright, we dare to dream,
A doughnut's glaze, it's all a scheme.

As we mix and whisk away strife,
We bake the questions into life.
So lift your cake, let's cheer the ride,
With whisked delights, our hearts collide.

Cupcake Conundrums

Is it better sweet or savory?
Choose a cupcake, lose your worry.
Chocolate, vanilla, or lemon zest?
All the flavors put to the test.

When faced with trials, don't despair,
Just bake a cake, and show you care.
A sprinkle here, a cherry there,
Eat your worries, share a layer.

What if frosting dreams are lost?
Just grab the whipped cream, that's the cost.
In every layer, a story thrives,
With every cupcake, yum survives!

So when you ponder what's the key,
Remember cupcakes, and you'll see.
A conundrum's solved with each sweet bite,
A tasty puzzle, pure delight.

A Slice of Wisdom

A slice of wisdom, what's the scoop?
With pie or cake, join the loop.
Life's a party, so slice it right,
One wedge of joy, a glowing light.

Should you go for fudge or pie?
Just grab a fork and give a try.
The crowded table speaks so loud,
Dessert is king, we sing it proud.

When questions linger, we ask--why?
With every bite, the answers fly.
The frosting thick, the crust so thin,
With every dessert, let's dive right in.

So savor crumbs, don't let them fall,
In every bite, there's truth for all.
A slice of cake, a twist of fate,
With sprinkles on top, we celebrate!

The Frosting on Existence

What's the meaning? Just take a taste,
With frosting smooth, make haste, make haste!
Life's thick layer, so sweet and fair,
Eat it up without a care.

Questions swirl like sugar spun,
Yet frosting's here, let's have some fun.
Should we laugh, or should we cry?
Just grab a cupcake, give it a try.

When the world feels bitter-sweet,
A slice of cake is quite the treat.
Within the layers, truth's unfurled,
Frosting brings joy to this crazy world.

So when in doubt, just take a bite,
Finding answers in every light.
The frosting's thick but brings a twist,
In every gobble, there's bliss to list.

Crumbs of Clarity

With crumbs of clarity, let's explore,
Each morsel brimming with wisdom's core.
What's the secret behind the cake?
In every slice, a chance to wake.

Should we worry about our ways?
Or dance with cake on sunny days?
Each sprinkle tells a silly tale,
Of frosting dreams that never fail.

When life gets tough, and hearts feel low,
Just whip up sweetness, let it flow.
In every bite, a smile found,
With every crumb, joy's profound.

So gather round, bring out the pies,
With laughter echoing to the skies.
Crumbs of clarity in every feast,
In the joy of sweets, we find our peace.

Slices of Serenity

When worries swirl, and thoughts collide,
I turn to sweets, a sugary guide.
A slice of vanilla, so smooth and bright,
With frosting dreams to make it right.

Questions linger in the air,
But chocolate mousse, oh, I don't care!
A sprinkle of laughter, a dash of fun,
In cake, my friend, we become one.

Should I leap, or play it safe?
Just grab a fork, and let's escape!
With every bite, oh joyous thrill,
I ponder fate with dessert-filled will.

So as the world spins fast and wild,
I find my peace just like a child.
In layers rich, my thoughts unwind,
In sweet indulgence, calm I find.

Conundrums in Carrot Cake

Carrots in cake? Who thought it right?
A puzzling dish, a curious sight.
Is it healthy? Is it sweet?
Or just a way the veggies sneak treat?

Can frosting hide my doubts and fears?
Just one more piece to dry my tears.
I fork it up, it's quite the blend,
Life's quirky plots around the bend.

Is this a snack, or a new philosophy?
With every slice, I seek a remedy.
Nutty bits of wisdom I find,
In cream cheese swirls, answers unwind.

Or is it just icing on the cake?
Confusion frosted, but that's no mistake.
With every bite, doubts dance and sway,
Carrot cake, oh lead the way!

Biscuit Bound Decisions

Should I crumble, should I stand?
In biscuits round, I find my brand.
A buttery crunch hides secret calls,
With every dunk, my courage falls.

Tea or coffee? I cannot choose,
But ginger snaps will never lose.
A flaky bite brings joy, you see,
In crumbs of solace, I'll just be free.

Decisions swirl like frosting thick,
With biscuits round, I take my pick.
Scones so light, or shortbread strong?
Each taste a lyric, a flavor song.

So bake it proud, with laughter bright,
In biscuit land, I'll find my light.
With every crunch, the world feels right,
Doughy dreams take flight tonight.

Whips and Whisks of Wisdom

Whisking thoughts like batter so light,
Stirring worries away, out of sight.
With every whip, the chaos sings,
In bowls of joy, each laughter springs.

Should I be bold? Should I just blend?
In meringue, I seek a friend.
Tender peaks of fluffy dreams,
My soul revives in sweetened streams.

With every fold, I gain insight,
A dash of fun makes all things right.
Cream and sugar, life's great tease,
In cake, I find my inner ease.

Whisk away doubt, let joy arise,
In layers rich, the answer lies.
With whips and whisks, I shall explore,
In baking's magic, I want more!

Batter of Beliefs

In a bowl of dreams, we stir and mix,
With flour of hopes, and sugar tricks.
The eggs of wisdom crack with glee,
    Together we bake our recipe!

Can chocolate solve the world's great pain?
Or will vanilla reign supreme, the bane?
Add sprinkles of laughter, a pinch of fun,
    A slice of joy makes all hearts run.

What's the secret to the quest of fate?
Is it buttercream or just to wait?
With each layer stacked, we ponder still,
    For every slice, we eat our fill.

When doubts arise like crumbs in tea,
Let's serve them warm, with glee, just three.
In the oven of chance, we take our bets,
    And laugh with frosting, no regrets!

Sugary Solutions

When troubles bubble, what's the fix?
A cupcake charm or frosted tricks?
Carrot cake for the healthy folks,
With frosting piled high—it's all a hoax!

Is there guidance in a slice of pie?
Or is the wisdom in the rye?
We toss our fears like flour in air,
With buttery hopes, we don't despair.

Here's the answer, it's sweet and thick,
Layer our doubts, make them slick.
With icing smiles and cherry cheer,
We bake our truths, year after year.

So grab a fork, it's time to bite,
In sugary tales, we find delight.
From cookies' crunch to tarts divine,
The answers lie where we dine!

Tiers of Truths

In layers stacked, we find our thoughts,
A cake so tall, with sprinkles caught.
Beneath the frosting, secrets hide,
With every slice, we turn the tide.

What's found in fondant, soft and grand?
A truth so sweet, you'll understand.
The tiered delights of every slice,
Bring laughter forth, oh, isn't it nice?

Let's bake a cake for all our fears,
With butter and cream, let's spread the cheers.
Each candle lit, a new year's wish,
For every taste, a heavenly dish.

As we devour, we ponder why,
Is it cake that keeps our spirits high?
For every bite, a question fades,
In layers of bliss, all doubts are laid!

Frosting the Unknown

What's lurking deep in the batter's core?
Mysteries swirl—should we explore?
With frosting knives, we spread our fears,
A sprinkle of hope drowns all our tears.

When life gets hard, just bake a thing,
A pie, a tart, hear laughter ring.
Is cherry jubilee the key to peace?
Or perhaps a brownie will bring release?

The cookies may crumble, the loaf may flop,
But every mishap, we flip and swap.
With each big slice, our troubles shrink,
In dessert and joy, we dare to think.

So when unsure, let's whip and fold,
For in each recipe, a story's told.
Frosting the mystery, sweet delight,
Together we bake through day and night!

Sweet Tooth Reflection

When wondering what's the meaning,
I bake a chocolate dream!
A slice of gooey goodness,
Life's questions taste like cream.

Each forkful brings a smile,
As frosting melts my doubts.
With sprinkles on the side,
I ponder what it's about.

A cupcake's whims will guide me,
Through existential dread.
I'll take a bite of strawberry,
And crave what's in my head.

So here's to tasty answers,
In layers we explore.
In every sweet encounter,
Life's mysteries we score.

The Ponderings of Pastry

Whisking up my wild thoughts,
In batter, they take flight.
When pie crust holds my worries,
I bake them out of sight.

Chocolate ganache whispers,
Secrets of the day.
A mousse of endless questions,
May help to find the way.

With every doughnut's shape,
There's meaning to my strife.
A cherry on the topping,
Suggests a sweeter life.

As cookies crumble nicely,
I crumble with delight.
In every scrumptious moment,
I'm soaring to new heights.

Sifting Through Uncertainties

Sifting flour through my fingers,
I question every grain.
What's the purpose of this journey?
In muffins I find gain.

A pinch of salt for wisdom,
A dash of sugar's cheer.
In every baked creation,
New insight draws me near.

Tarts remind me of balance,
With fillings rich and bright.
I ponder cosmic wonders,
While munching without fright.

So let's toast with cupcakes,
To life's mysterious bake.
In frosting, I find answers,
A sugary heartache.

Flour Power Questions

What's the secret ingredient,
To joy within a day?
A cookie's soft embrace,
Can chase my woes away.

In muffins dense with questions,
I find a tasty pause.
I slice through every worry,
With icing as my cause.

With layers stacked like moments,
I ponder crusty doubts.
Each bite brings revelation,
Slicing through my routes.

So let's gather for cake talks,
With frosting on the side.
In every crumb, a story,
And in pastries, I confide.

The Cakewalk of Thought

Whisked dreams float in the air,
With sprinkles of hope everywhere.
Each layer stacked, a wish unfurled,
In frosting swirls, we taste the world.

Questions rise like dough in heat,
While chocolate makes the bitter sweet.
Is this the secret, or just a tease?
Let's slice the cake, and take it, please!

Wisdom baked, we pull a slice,
Is happiness just a bit of spice?
With forks in hand, the truth we map,
Life's better served with a tasty flap.

So let us ponder as we chew,
With every bite, a kernel of truth.
Unlock the mysteries in pie crust,
And pass the cake, we'll figure the rest!

Conundrums in Cream

What's the answer to the riddle, dear?
Is frosting thick, our greatest fear?
If we can't see what's hidden beneath,
Do we just eat, and savor the wreath?

With layers stacked, we ponder and bake,
Can buttercream solve the whims we make?
Does sugar sweeten the bitter fight,
Or just color dreams in pastel light?

In each spongy bite, a truth appears,
Lifting our spirits, calming our fears.
Is it all just fluff, marzipan gloss?
Or does cake hold wisdom, not just loss?

Let's dig deep into that spongey core,
Glimpsing truths that we can't ignore.
And if life's questions do twist and whirl,
I'll take the cake, and give it a twirl!

Tasting the Truth

Cake is the answer, that's what they say,
Why ponder too much at the end of the day?
A slice of jam, a scoop of lore,
With every bite, we find out more.

Creamy laughter fills the air,
As chocolate chips find their soulful pair.
Is this the meaning or just dessert?
Oh, take a fork, escape the hurt!

With layers thick and flavors bold,
Do we find solace in what we hold?
Each bite's an answer, sweet and clear,
Reminding us why we're all still here.

So let's toast with cake to the unknown,
In frosting tales, we've brightly grown.
Tasting delight, we smile and sing,
For answers may be just a cake away, zing!

The Revelations of Roulade

Roll up the questions with a fun twist,
What's the best flavor? Pumpkin or mist?
As we slice through the layers of thought,
Let's savor what the pastry has brought.

With every twist, a surprise we meet,
Is frosting or filling the true heart's beat?
In the dance of desserts, we find our way,
Chasing crumbs, we seize the day.

Do we seek wisdom in the cake we bake?
Or does every crumb just lead to a break?
With each bite taken, we ponder anew,
Maybe the answers were hidden in goo.

So here's to the roulade, both sweet and sly,
Life's mysteries wrapped up, oh my, oh my!
With laughter and cake, we boldly tread,
Finding truths with frosting, our spirits fed!

Whisked Away Insights

What is the meaning of the bake?
Flour power, for goodness' sake!
Whisk up your dreams, sprinkle them fair,
Taste life's sweetness, if you dare.

Cherries on top, a frosted thought,
Mixing struggles that can't be bought.
Slice through doubts with a cake knife,
A crumbly truth, the secret of life.

Can friendship rise like soufflé fluff?
With butter and sugar, it's never tough.
Bake together through thick and thin,
For frosting's the joy we keep within.

Do calories count in the grand scheme?
Maybe, but chocolate's still a dream.
Live and let bake, and laugh away,
As crumbs of whimsy lead the way.

A Confectioner's Philosophy

What's the secret to joy, you ask?
It's layers of cake, a delightful task.
Slice away woes, let laughter spread,
With crumbs of wisdom on your bread.

Is there a shortcut to fleeting bliss?
Only if frosting's what you miss.
Whip up some creams, and shade that gray,
In the vanilla bean of everyday.

How do we cope with the bitter spins?
Sugar and spice, that's how life begins.
Mix in a joke, let the batter roll,
Finding the sweet will fill up your soul.

Why do we bake in a world so wild?
To gather the loved and inspire the child.
Every cupcake holds a memory snug,
In the kitchen's heart, we steam with a hug.

Cake Layers of Understanding

Why does the world keep spinning 'round?
Like layers of cake, we're tightly bound.
Sift out the doubts, let laughter thrive,
For icing rich helps us survive.

What defines success, a win or slice?
A fork in hand, and oh, so nice.
Savor the joy, let the forks collide,
In the bakery of dreams, we confide.

What's the recipe for depth and fun?
Mix laughter with love, until it's done.
A sprinkle here, a dash of that,
The sweeter the cake, the better the chat.

Is life just a thing to be devoured?
No, it's the frosting that leaves us empowered.
So stack up the layers, let's take a chance,
In the dance of flavors, we all prance.

The Icing of Introspection

What are we made of, if not cake?
With sprinkles of hope, we merrily wake.
Crumb by crumb, we discover our fate,
In layers of laughter, we create.

Is there more to this sweetened path?
It's frosting that softens our aftermath.
Peering deep into the creamy swirl,
Life's a confection, let it unfurl.

What do you do when the cake goes flat?
Add some more sugar and swing the spat!
Lick the bowl, take a moment to cheer,
For every mishap, a dessert's near.

Will we ever learn all the tricks?
Perhaps through baking, we'll solve the fix.
Sprinkle some joy with every bake done,
In the oven of thought, we'll always run.

Ganache of Growth

With chocolate so rich, we ponder our fate,
A slice of delight, we just can't wait.
Layers of frosting, sweet truths we find,
Life's little lessons are better defined.

From crumbs of our past, we bake something new,
With sprinkles of joy, and a dash of rue.
Each tier tells a story, soft, moist, and bold,
In the oven of time, our dreams unfold.

So when things get tough, take a bite from the pan,
For cake is the answer, or so says the plan.
In gooey confessions, with layers galore,
We laugh at the questions, and ask the world for more.

Flour fights, icing spills, in chaos we thrive,
With cakes on our tables, we surely arrive.
So let's raise our forks, and feast on delight,
For the ganache of growth feels perfectly right.

Cakewalk to Enlightenment

Strolling through frosting, so sweet and divine,
A cakewalk to wisdom, one slice at a time.
With sprinkles of laughter, we dance in the light,
As we nibble on questions, it all feels so right.

Fluffy and fun, the layers unwind,
In icing, we find the truth of mankind.
We giggle with joy over crumbs of old lore,
For each forkful reveals just a bit more.

The batter of life, a mix of good cheer,
Whisked with the moments that bring us near.
So let's savor the sweetness, and frolic around,
In the cakewalk of wisdom, pure happiness found.

With cake as our guide on this whimsical quest,
We bake up the answers, and have ourselves blessed.
So take a big slice, let the fun not take flight,
In this cakewalk to wisdom, all flavors feel right.

Pastry Paradoxes

In ovens of wonder, where dreams take their bake,
We ponder the questions inside each big cake.
The crust may be tough, but the inside is sweet,
In pastries of life, we find answers to meet.

For every fondant, a mystery swirls,
With layers of wisdom, our laughter unfurls.
Like eclairs that puff, we rise with a cheer,
While tarts tease our taste buds, and draw us near.

With cherries on top, paradoxes blend,
For happiness blooms, just like pastry does mend.
Let's fork through the layers of gooey delight,
And chuckle at life as we savor each bite.

So here's to the pastries that lead us astray,
In the kitchen of giggles, we happily play.
Life's quirks are like marzipan, sweet and absurd,
In the pastry of questions, get ready for word!

Morsels of Meaning

In every small crumb, there's a riddle to stir,
A bite-sized delight, as our minds gently purr.
With cookies and cream, we munch on the wise,
As we laugh 'til we cry, drowning doubts in the pies.

Each morsel of cake hides a secret or two,
In layers of laughter, we discover what's true.
From cupcakes to brownies, life's flavors combine,
With sprinkles of joy, the answers align.

So let's chew on the nonsense, and swallow it down,
With frosting so fitting, we'll dance all around.
In this banquet of questions, we feast on delight,
In morsels of laughter, it all feels so right.

For every slice taken, a smile will arise,
Like cakes at a party, we search for the prize.
So grab a good fork, and come join in the fun,
In this dessert of existence, we'll never be done.

The Tiers of Existence

In layers thick, we seek our fate,
Biting into joy, we contemplate.
Chocolate or vanilla, what will it be?
Questions rise like icing, sweet and free.

With every slice, a mystery unfolds,
Do we eat to live, or live to hold?
A fork in hand, we reach for more,
As each crumb crumbles, we explore.

What's the meaning of this fluffy cream?
Is it delight, or just a dream?
We laugh at frosting's whimsical sway,
As we devour the doubts that play.

So grab a plate, let's share our cake,
Each bite takes us further on this break.
In sugar and pastry, life's lessons stir,
Who knew that cake could raise a blur?

Taste of Contemplation

A cupcake's wit, so sublime and sweet,
As we ponder if we're truly complete.
Is frosting the answer to all our woes?
Or just a distraction that nobody knows?

In dough we trust, it rises and spins,
Barely holding all our hopes within.
Carrot, or red velvet, which path to choose?
Decisions are tough, but what's there to lose?

A hint of spice, a dash of cheer,
Life's questions linger, but never fear.
With sprinkles of laughter all over the tray,
We munch on our doubts and laugh them away.

As men ask who, and women just why,
We bake up answers, oh my, oh my!
In every slice, a giggle and sigh,
For cake is our muse, under frosted sky.

Frosted Reflections

In the mirror of icing, we see our plight,
Reflecting on choices, the day and the night.
Do we bake with care or just dive right in?
With spatulas ready, let the fun begin!

Each layer we stack, our wisdom unfolds,
Like candles on top, our stories retold.
Are we the baker or just a mere crumb?
In the kitchen of questions, we all feel numb.

Shall we chew on the fears that crunch like a pie?
With whimsy and humor, we spread caution to fly.
For baked goods unite, in celebrations and tears,
And frosting is sweeter when shared with peers.

So let's slice our cake, with smiles so wide,
While asking for sprinkles to join in our ride.
The answers are baked in the laughter we share,
In frosted reflections, we find love and care.

The Pastry Path to Answers

On a buttery journey through muffin-filled roads,
Each pastry a compass, each crumb a code.
A croissant's twist holds the secrets of fun,
While scones tease the answers, one by one.

Can we frost our worries, or bake them today?
Each layer a story, in a delightful array.
With buttercream dreams floating through the air,
The oven is warm, and so is our care.

As we nibble on doubts, they crumble like pie,
A giggle escapes with each heartfelt sigh.
Do answers lie baked in this doughy delight?
Or are we just wandering through layers of light?

So dance with the whisk, and swirl with those tarts,
For pastry holds wisdom, it warms our hearts.
Each bite brings a chuckle, a truth, and a grin,
Who knew that sweet treats had life tucked within?

Teetering on Tarts

When baking's a puzzle, what's the fix?
A pie in the oven, or a few silly tricks?
Life's flaky crust, it crumbles and sways,
But sweeter it feels with each sugary phase.

A sprinkle of joy, a dab of despair,
Just whip up a frosting, what do you care?
If tarts tip over, who's keeping score?
With laughter and crumbs, who could want more?

The layers in life, some bitter, some sweet,
Like chocolate on cupcakes, a marvelous treat!
Take each slice boldly, with a grin on your face,
For happiness sizzles in this sugar-filled space.

So stack up your pastries, let's bring out the cheer,
For pastries may waver, but laughter is here!
In the kitchen of life, let's bake and let rise,
With meringue on our heads, we tackle the skies!

Answering the Bake-off of Existence

In the oven of thoughts, what rises so high?
Is it wisdom or chocolate? Oh me, oh my!
With flour as proof, we whip up our fate,
And sprinkle on love, it's never too late.

Riddles of rising, cakes puffing with pride,
Each layer a secret we cannot abide.
Sifting through questions, we find our delight,
A cupcake for clarity, oh what a sight!

Do brownies hold answers, or just sticky goo?
With a scoop of vanilla, we make do!
From frosting to fondant, we dress it just right,
Like icing on problems, they shine in the light.

Embrace the bake-off, don't fear the unknown,
For baking's a mystery, but you're not alone!
Let's whisk up some laughter, it's never a chore,
In this sweet little battle, we'll always want more!

The Ganache Gaze

Gazing into ganache, the world seems so bright,
Is it love, or chocolate? Both feel just right!
With a spoon in hand, we ponder and dream,
While cocoa and whispers merge in one gleam.

In layers of flavor, we seek out the truth,
Are sprinkles of wisdom a cake's hidden proof?
If frosting could talk, how sweet would it say,
To savor each moment in a frosted ballet?

With buttercream wishes, we gather around,
For cake's not just cake, it's joy that we've found!
A bite of our thoughts, they melt on the tongue,
In this decadent dance, we feel ever young.

So ponder on fancies, and melt in the thrill,
For each bite of cake gives the heart a good fill.
Life's contemplations, dipped in sweet glaze,
In the ganache of laughter, we find our own ways!

Flavorful Dilemmas

When faced with decisions, should it be pie?
Or a towering layer cake reaching the sky?
With flavors of chaos, we slice through the mess,
A tart filled with questions, oh what a quest!

Should we bake it with confidence, or add a few sprinkles?
What if the frosting just shrivels and crinkles?
Whisk in some humor, and if all else fails,
We're left with a cupcake that happily wails.

In the jungle of ovens, where muffins abound,
Are their flavors of joy just waiting to be found?
With ganache on top, we take our big leap,
And savor the laughter in battles we keep.

So when doubts arise, just think of the cake,
For each sweet creation, a memory to make.
In this flavorful dance, let's embrace and extend,
For life's tasty troubles are best shared with a friend!

Pillars of Pound Cake Philosophy

What is the meaning of all this fuss?
Is it really just crumbs on the bus?
A slice of happiness, rich and dense,
Pound cake makes sense, it's just common sense.

In a world where layers can all confuse,
I seek frosting, for that's what I choose.
Is it buttercream? Or maybe chilled whip?
With cake in hand, I'm on a fun trip.

When questions arise like bubbles in tea,
I nibble on layers, and I feel so free.
Does joy come from taste or the friends that we bake?
I assert, with conviction, it's all about cake!

So here are my thoughts on the mysteries sweet,
With every good forkful, the world feels complete.
Life's secrets unravel, in each crumb and taste,
With a cake at the table, there's never a waste.

Confections of Curiosity

Do we dwell on the past like a stale old pie?
Or rise high as soufflés, unfazed by the sky?
Is frosting the answer when troubles abound?
Just a sprinkle of sugar can turn it around.

When pondering flavors in a cookie spree,
Do we find our direction in a sweet cup of tea?
Is a brownie a friend or a foe to the heart?
In the game of desserts, we all play a part.

With each sugary bite, there's a question that flows,
Does chocolate bring peace? Oh, the joy it bestows!
As sprinkles scatter, we ponder and chew,
I conclude that life's better with frosting in view.

Let's gather our forks 'round the cake and the pie,
In laughter and crumbs, let the worries just fly.
Curiosity answered with laughter and cheer,
In the realm of desserts, there's nothing to fear.

The Enigma of Éclairs

What's the secret to joy in a Paris delight?
Is it custard or glaze that keeps shining so bright?
We ponder and taste as we savor the cream,
Life's questions dissolve like an éclair's sweet dream.

If chocolate's the answer to every dark thought,
Then calories vanish, or so I have sought.
With pastry and pastry, our minds start to blend,
The more we indulge, the less we pretend.

Do éclairs hold wisdom in each layered bite?
With a flick of our forks, we reach for the light.
In a world of confusion, a crisp crunch in hand,
We've solved the great mysteries of this yummy land.

One final conclusion, as we fix our tableau,
It's a laugh and a bite that make fortunes bestow.
So share all your pastries, and let's raise a cheer,
In the enigma of éclairs, happiness is near!

A Delicate Dough of Debate

Is the crust worth the fight or too flaky to save?
Does butter or oil make the best kind of wave?
With pastries around, does it matter who's right?
In the oven of chat, every question takes flight.

Are muffins just cupcakes, in disguise or for show?
When filling's involved, does it matter? We know!
The sweetness of dough can soften the strife,
In the bakery of banter, we taste the good life.

Shall we whip up a storm while we ponder the pie?
Or are crumbs all that's left as we laugh, oh my,
With flavors combined, we declare that we're friends,
The debates can be silly, but happiness blends.

So let's raise our forks to the questions, dear friend,
In the kitchen of taste, there's no way to pretend.
With each bite we share, we grow wiser, you see,
In this delicate dough, we find harmony!

Baked Truths

Why is the sky so blue, we ask,
Just slice some cake, it's quite the task.
Frosting thick, the answer's sweet,
Each crumb a truth, a tasty treat.

When asking why the world is round,
Just take a bite, and look around.
With every layer, clarity grows,
In every piece, a wisdom shows.

To know what's next, just eat a slice,
For frosting offers sage advice.
So grab a fork, dig into this lore,
In cake, you'll find what you're looking for.

And if you're feeling lost and blue,
Remember cake has all the clues.
With every morsel, laugh and cheer,
For cake will always draw you near.

The Sugar Coated Dilemmas

Do we take the leap, or play it safe?
Ask the cupcake, it's the best waif.
With sprinkles bright and frosting high,
It knows the way, oh me, oh my!

When faced with choices, sweet and strange,
Just look to cake, it won't change.
Layered like thoughts, rich and grand,
Each bite will guide you, just understand!

Is it better to be thin or round?
The cupcake says to stand your ground.
With cream-filled hearts and doughy dreams,
It promises joy, or so it seems.

So when in doubt, take a big bite,
For cake's insights are pure delight.
With every flavor, every taste,
Find laughter first, then wisdom's haste.

Decadent Decisions

Should we go left or take a right?
Just munch on cake, it feels so light.
With chocolate rivers and vanilla skies,
You'll find the answer in sugary highs.

When pondering what to do today,
A slice of pie will pave the way.
Crust so flaky, filling divine,
Decisions become a sweet align.

Do we conquer fear or play it cool?
A cake says dance, life's a sweet school.
With frosting bold and flavors wide,
Take a big bite, let joy be your guide.

And in the end, when choices loom,
Remember cake can sweeten gloom.
With every bite, the fun's enhanced,
In pastry, you'll find true romance!

Recipes for Resolve

What's the secret to a life well-lived?
A dash of cake, that's how it's given.
Mix laughter well, and honey too,
Bake it gently; it's a recipe for you!

In times of doubt, what should we do?
Frosting whispers, 'Open the view.'
Add in some sprinkles, a dash of zest,
For cake will tell what you love best.

Should we follow dreams or play it safe?
Grab a cookie, and turn the page.
With crumbs beneath and icing above,
You'll find the path that fits like a glove.

So when life's conundrums come to call,
Remember, cake can answer all.
With each sweet layer, a truth unfolds,
For every heart, let the sweetness hold!

The Cake that Knows

Why ponder the stars when sprinkles abound?
Slice it just right, and truth can be found.
Layers of frosting, wisdom-packed tight,
In every sweet bite, darkness turns bright.

Chocolate or vanilla, what's better for fate?
Choose wisely, my friend, before it's too late.
The answer's in buttercream, fluffy and sweet,
Each forkful a lesson, a delicious treat.

When life gives you lemons, bake up a pie!
Lemon meringue for questions that fly.
A slice served with laughter, joy in the air,
With cake by your side, you've nothing to fear.

So let's raise our forks, let curiosity reign,
For cake holds the secrets, and that's not in vain.
With each tasty bite, we ponder and play,
The cake that knows all, in its own special way.

Confections of Understanding

What's the meaning of life in a cupcake's swirl?
Frosting philosophies that brightly unfurl.
Sprinkle it lightly with laughter and cheer,
In confections we trust; the answer is clear.

Baked goods unite us in flaky delight,
From cookies to cakes, we revel in bite.
Chocolate chip dreams or a sweet raspberry twist,
In layers of pastries, we find what we've missed.

Questions like bubbles, they rise with the heat,
In ovens of wonder, we savor the sweet.
The truth's in the dough, so knead it with glee,
With pastries of wisdom, we're set to be free.

So slice up the wonder, the joy of the feast,
In crumbs of delight, we worry the least.
Life may be puzzling, but here's the decree:
With cakes in your corner, laugh heartily!

Icing on the Inquiry

What lies beyond clouds, in layers of cream?
Frosting top secrets, that's just my dream.
With a cake as my guide, I'm set for the quest,
It whispers a riddle, and I'm truly blessed.

Is joy just a layer, fluffy and sweet?
Or is it a crumble, that's hard to beat?
With every sweet nibble, I ponder and play,
The icing on questions will brighten the day.

When things get too heavy, just bake for a while,
Whip up a soufflé and let life bring a smile.
With frosting doodles, my worries take flight,
In confections of longing, all feels just right.

So let's celebrate answers, in dessert we trust,
Adding humor to queries, it's truly a must.
With sugar and laughter, we'll dance in delight,
For the icing brings wisdom, and makes wrongs feel right.

Whipped Dreams and Realities

In the kitchen of wonder, dreams take their shape,
Whipped cream for questions, frosting escapes.
Is life just a bake-off, judging our hearts?
Or a rich layer cake where each flavor imparts?

What's the recipe for happiness, pray tell?
Is it caramel drizzle or chocolate as well?
I argue with brownies, so rich, so divine,
In the chat of confections, we sip and we dine.

When doubts start to linger and worries arise,
Pie charts of pastries can open our eyes.
Each bite is a journey, a whimsical ride,
With whipped cream realities resting inside.

So gather your friends and let cake be the key,
To questions unfurling like blossoms on a tree.
In layers of laughter, we find what we seek,
For sweet dreams wrapped in frosting are perfect and meek.

Fueled by Fondant

What's the secret to happiness?
A slice of chocolate bliss.
With sprinkles on the top,
You can't go wrong like this.

Why worry about your cares?
Just bake a lemon tart.
With icing that declares,
You've truly got the art.

Is time just a fleeting myth?
Count layers in a cake.
One bite and you'll be sure
That seconds are at stake.

What makes the world rotate?
It's buttercream divine.
And while you contemplate,
Just pass me that red wine.

The Artisan's Inquiry

Why chase the grandest goals?
When cookies call my name.
Each frosting swirl consoles,
And drowns my doubts in fame.

Is fortune just a dream?
A cupcake can suffice.
I'll take it with some cream,
Or maybe once or twice.

What's love? The sweetest blend?
A pie that's shared with you.
With crumbles, one could mend,
Relationships, that's true.

What's the meaning of it all?
A slice of cake, I say.
If life starts to feel small,
Just bake your blues away.

Savoring the Unknown

What comes next after this?
A cupcake on my plate.
With sprinkles, I can kiss
The worries that await.

Is patience a virtue here?
Then let's ice a cake slow.
With every layer near,
It's swifter than you know.

Will dreams just bake away?
Or rise like fluffy dough?
Let's mix a bit of play,
And see just where we go.

What's the key to it all?
A brownie's warm embrace.
In sweetness, I shall fall,
And find my happy place.

Heartfelt Ingredients

What stirs the soul profound?
A pie just out of sight.
With every slice I've found,
I'm served a piece of light.

Do questions fade in time?
Or soften like a cake?
With frosting's gentle rhyme,
We ponder, stir, and bake.

What's life without some zest?
A tart that's keenly bright.
So let's indulge the quest,
With pastries, all feels right.

What matters at the core?
Is it butter, flour, fun?
Just bake a little more,
And let the laughter run.

Desserting the Doubts

When worries rise like frosting peaks,
I grab a slice, and silence speaks.
Each crumb a friend, each bite a cheer,
What's sweeter than cake to quell your fear?

The answer lies in chocolate's flow,
A decadent truth we all should know.
With sprinkles of joy, and layers of cream,
What's life's grand plan? Just eat and dream!

A hint of tart in a lemon cake,
Reminds me that not all is at stake.
When doubts arise like burnt soufflés,
I simply bake; I'll find my ways!

The Flour of Fate

In bowls of flour, the odds we knead,
Butter and sugar, the ultimate creed.
Do cakes predict what fate may bring?
Or just an excuse to eat and sing?

A sprinkle of chaos, a dash of fun,
Whisk up your worries; let's not be done!
With icing on top, the answers are sweet,
Roll with the punches, and life's a treat!

Pondering with Pastries

Croissants whisper secrets, flaky and light,
About choices made in the dead of night.
Doughnuts spin tales on crispy wheels,
Sprinkled wisdom comes from how it feels.

When muffins rise, so do our hopes,
With every bake, our spirit copes.
What to do when the oven's closed?
Find sweet delight, by fate, we're posed!

Eclair the Unknown

In the depths of pastries, truths reside,
With a crème-filled heart, let worries slide.
Sift through the shadows, catch a glimpse,
Eclairs hold answers, they never skimp.

When faced with puzzles, there's one true fix,
A pastry so rich, it's a tasty mix.
With every bite, let laughter reign,
For in the pastry shop, nothing's plain!

Slices of Wisdom

A chocolate layer looks so wise,
With every bite, a sweet surprise.
If life gets tough, just grab a slice,
For frosting thick, oh, isn't nice!

Each crumb reveals a secret truth,
Vanilla dreams and sprinkles of youth.
When questions come, just take a taste,
Forget the rush, there's no need for haste.

Frosted Philosophies

A pie of thoughts, frosted bright,
What's the meaning? Take a bite!
With layers deep and a cherry on top,
It's all about fun; just never stop!

Why ponder hard? Just grab some cake,
Each flavor says, 'For goodness' sake!'
Chocolate declares, 'Live in the now,'
While fruitcake smirks, 'Take a bow!'

Sweet Resolutions

On New Year's Eve, what do we vow?
More cake, less time for the how.
Each bite suggests, 'Go take a chance!',
In frosting's dance, we find romance.

Minty fresh, like hopes anew,
Layered dreams for me and you.
So when you fret, just grab a fork,
And savor joy; come on, let's gawk!

Layers of Existence

In custard's heart, deep questions hide,
Pastry crisp, with dreams inside.
A cupcake muses, 'What's our fate?'
While pie just laughs, 'Let's celebrate!'

Each layer tells a funny tale,
Of ups and downs, of wind and hail.
So take a slice, let worries flee,
In every crumb, find jubilee!

Sprinkles of Serenity

What's the meaning of this bliss?
Some frosting on a cheeky kiss.
With each bite, we ponder more,
Cake's the answer we explore.

Flavors mix and blend so sweet,
Cherry pie and chocolate treat.
In layers deep, we find the truth,
Dessert for wisdom, joy, and youth.

With sprinkles bright, we chart our fate,
Cheesecake dreams on a silver plate.
A slice to share, no need to fear,
We're laughing loud while eating here.

So when you ask what life's about,
Grab a fork and join the shout!
For in each crumb, a clue does lie,
Cake is wisdom—we cannot deny!

Carving the Conundrum

What's swirling in the cosmic pie?
Is it lemon, or is it lie?
Let's grab a knife, let's slice it thin,
Decoding life with chocolate grin.

Each layer tells a tasty tale,
Of frosting hills and vanilla veil.
Questions rise like soufflés high,
So let's indulge and just comply.

What's the secret? It's easy, friend,
A cake for thought 'til flavors blend.
With every bite, the puzzle's clear,
Bake and taste, no need for fear.

In cake we trust, let's share a slice,
A giggle-mix of sugar and spice.
For every problem, there's a cake,
So grab a fork, for goodness' sake!

The Slice of Serenity

What's hidden in this doughy coil?
A scoop of joy, a dash of toil.
Grab your fork, it's time to choose,
Does wisdom hide in chocolate mousse?

Is there meaning in the mint?
With every crumb, we take a hint.
As frosted branches reach the sky,
Questions float like pie birds high.

What's the trick to all we seek?
A cupcake here, a donut peak.
Life's a bake-off in the end,
With frosting friends around the bend.

So let us laugh and munch away,
Each slice reveals a bright new day.
In sugar-coated truths we trust,
Cake's the key—it's simply just!

Cake Crumbs and Cosmos

What's beyond the sprinkles bright?
A universe of cake delight.
With every bite, we ponder deep,
What stellar secrets cake might keep?

Is the frosting made from stars?
Or just a treat from Mars to ours?
With crumbs that fall like whispered dreams,
In icing lies the sweetest schemes.

Do answers hide in lemon zest?
Or maybe vanilla is the best?
Slice by slice, we delve and seek,
With every taste, we gain the peak.

So let us raise our forks in cheer,
To crumbs that bring the cosmos near.
In this sweet quest, we laugh and play,
For cake reveals our goofy way!

www.ingramcontent.com/pod-product-compliance
Lightning Source LLC
Chambersburg PA
CBHW051655160426
43209CB00004B/911